101 449 425 7

KNOWABOUT

Size

© 1994 Watts Books

Watts Books
96 Leonard Street
London EC2A 4RH

Franklin Watts Australia
14 Mars Road
Lane Cove
NSW 2066

ISBN: 0 7496 1734 9

Dewey Decimal Classification: 516

10 9 8 7 6 5 4 3 2 1

A CIP catalogue record for this book
is available from the British Library.

Editor: Ruth Thomson
Assistant Editor: Annabel Martin

Design: Chloë Cheesman

Additional photographs: Chris Fairclough
Colour Library © Andrew Rapacz 28;
The Natural History Museum, London 12, 13;
ZEFA 26.

Printed in Hong Kong

KNOWABOUT

Size

Text: Henry Pluckrose
Photography: Chris Fairclough

Watts Books
London • New York • Sydney

Do you ever wonder
what words mean?
This is a toy elephant.
It is so big
that it is difficult to carry.

This baby elephant
is bigger than the toy elephant,
but the mother elephant
is the biggest of them all.

This is a toy car.

How do you know that it is too small
to carry people?

This car looks similar to the toy car.

How can you tell that it is bigger?

This is a double decker bus.

It carries over 50 people.

It is bigger than the car

and the van.

It is the biggest vehicle of all.

To judge the size of things we need to have something to measure them against. These wheels could be of any size.

How do you know
that this wheel
is enormous?

It is hard to guess how large
this model might be.
Is it big – or is it small?

We know that this dinosaur is very big indeed!

These fruits are different sizes.

Which is the biggest?

Which is the smallest?

These toy bears are not the same size.

Which is bigger? Which is smaller?

Sometimes we need to arrange things in order of size.

These jars are different sizes.

Now they have been ordered by size.

The biggest jar is on the left.

The smallest jar is on the right.

We use the words big and small
to describe the size of things.

A rabbit is bigger
than a gerbil . . .

but smaller than a pony.

The pony is a big animal,
but it is smaller than a cart horse.

The words big and small
help us to compare
one thing with another.
A coat can be too big ...

or too small.
Is the girl too big
for the coat,
or is the coat too small
for the girl?

When we buy shoes
we have to make sure
that they are the right size ...

for the person who is to wear them.

Sometimes we need to make
things appear larger
so that we can see them more easily.
A hornet is a very small creature.
Enlarged, it looks like this.

These are raindrops on a leaf.

They have also been enlarged.

Sometimes things seem to be smaller
than they really are.
This aircraft looks quite small
when it is high in the sky.

When it is on the ground, it looks much bigger.

How do you know

that this house is big enough

for you to live in ...

and that this house has been built for dolls?

What is the biggest thing you can think of?

What is the smallest?

About this book

This book is designed for use in the home, playgroup and
infant school.

Mathematics is a part of the child's world. It is not just about
interpreting numbers or in mastering the tricks of addition
or multiplication. Mathematics is about *Ideas*. These ideas
(or concepts) have been developed over the centuries to
help explain particular qualities, such as size, weight,
height, as well as relationships and comparisons. Yet all
too often the important part which an understanding of
mathematics will play in a child's development is forgotten
or ignored.

Most adults can solve simple mathematical tasks by "doing
them in their head." For example you can probably add up
or subtract simple numbers without the need for counters,
beads or fingers. Young children find such abstractions
almost impossible to master. They need to see, talk, touch
and experiment.

The photographs in this book and the text which supports
them have been prepared with one major aim. They have
been chosen to encourage talk around topics which are
essentially mathematical. By talking with you, the young
reader will be helped to explore some of the central
concepts which underpin mathematics. It is upon an
understanding of these concepts that a child's future
mastery of mathematics will be built.

Henry Pluckrose